Making Willow Furniture

Three Women Share Their Art

Bim Willow®

Schiffer® Publishing Ltd

4880 Lower Valley Road, Atglen, Pennsylvania 19310

Contents

Library of Congress Control Number: 2008939985

Designed by Mark David Bowyer
Type set in Calligraphy421 BT / Zurich BT

ISBN: 978-0-7643-3249-4
Printed in China

Schiffer Books are available at special discounts for bulk purchases for sales promotions or premiums. Special editions, including personalized covers, corporate imprints, and excerpts can be created in large quantities for special needs. For more information contact the publisher:

Published by Schiffer Publishing Ltd.
4880 Lower Valley Road
Atglen, PA 19310
Phone: (610) 593-1777; Fax: (610) 593-2002
E-mail: Info@schifferbooks.com

For the largest selection of fine reference books on this and related subjects, please visit our web site at
www.schifferbooks.com
We are always looking for people to write books on new and related subjects. If you have an idea for a book please contact us at the above address.

This book may be purchased from the publisher.
Include $5.00 for shipping.
Please try your bookstore first.
You may write for a free catalog.

In Europe, Schiffer books are distributed by
Bushwood Books
6 Marksbury Ave.
Kew Gardens
Surrey TW9 4JF England
Phone: 44 (0) 20 8392-8585; Fax: 44 (0) 20 8392-9876
E-mail: info@bushwoodbooks.co.uk
Website: www.bushwoodbooks.co.uk
Free postage in the U.K., Europe; air mail at cost.

Introduction

I started offering workshops eight years ago and soon found out that 80% of my students were women between the ages of 35 and 65 — the average age being over 50. These women grew up during the age when there were strict lines of what women were supposed to do and what men were supposed to do — the age when women were to be in the home and not out in "a man's world and a man's work place."

Since then many things have changed. Though racism and sexism still exist, I am glad to say they are on the decline. Still, women rustic furniture makers tell me that when they are working at a show, they often hear "does your husband make this furniture?" Incredibly rustic furniture making is still thought to be a man's job. When female students come to me to take a class, many doubt if they can build a piece of furniture, but their passion to learn overcomes their fear of incapability. When they are finished, they stand back and say "I can't believe I made that." Taking their piece home, they get the same reaction from their friends and family.

It should not be a surprise that women are as capable in building rustic furniture as any man. In many indigenous tribes, it was, and still is, the women who built the hut and made the furniture — not the men. The term "craftsman" and "man made" are archaic terms. This is neither a man's trade nor a man's world — it is a world with much diversity and as humans, we are just a part of the overall picture. Rustic furniture is a human trade, and in this book the rustic furniture is "woman made."

I am happy to present to you Cassilda Brown, Jo Kilmer, and Amy Lansburg, three courageous women who punch holes in the walls of gender exclusion and incapability and build rustic furniture for their living.

—Bim Willow

A Tepee Chair

Cassilda Brown

I spent quite a lot of time outdoors as a child and I guess you could say I was a "woodsy" kind of kid. I always built forts and things with sticks and really just enjoyed exploring the natural world around me.

My first experience with building rustic furniture was building hickory chairs for Phil and Ryan Faircloth of Appalachian Rustic Furniture. Phil taught me to build a willow chair and that was that. I have been building willow furniture on my own ever since. I have taught several people to build furniture over the years, including my children, but mainly I work alone.

Cut to length.

The back legs are about 2" in diameter with a 24" finished length. Starting with a piece somewhat longer than that, square the end of one of the back legs.

Square one end of the other back leg, hold it up to the first to be sure that they are matched for diameter and general shape. When you are satisfied, cut the second leg to length.

Measure 24" and mark.

Bevel the bottom edge of the leg with a rasp. The keeps the outer bark from touching the ground and aids in the retention of the bark as it shrinks.

The front legs are also about 2" in diameter and have a finished length of 16". Follow the same process for preparing them as you did for the back legs. Square the bottom.

Measure and mark 16".

Cut to length ...

...and rasp the bottom edge.

Any knots...

...can also be rasped.

Thirteen 24″ rungs, rails, and stretchers are needed. Twelve are about 1-1/4" in diameter, and one somewhat narrower to go behind the front legs. Square one end.

Measure 24″ and chop to length.

The frame pieces are ready. There are two sets of legs, front and back, and 3 rungs per side.

Lay a set of front and back legs on the surface so their bottoms are aligned and they are about 18″ apart.

Measure up from the bottom about 3″ and mark with a pencil on both legs.

Align the bottom edge of the lower rung with the mark and center it between the legs. There should be some overlap at each end.

Lay the other pieces in place to see how they will fit.

Nail the lower rung in place.

Measure down from the top of the front leg 2″.

For the upper rung, use a piece that is very straight. Align the top of the upper rung with the mark, with a 1-1/2″ overhang.

Mark the back leg 12″ from the bottom. This will be the top edge of the upper rung on the back leg, giving the seat a gentle slope toward the back.

Align the upper rail to the marks...

...and nail it in place.

Nail in place. This should stabilize the side piece.

One side of the chair takes form. With only one nail at each joint, some adjustment is still possible.

Add a second nail at each joint.

Position the brace piece. Abut the front edge with the upper rail.

Use the finished side as a template for the other.

Mark and add the lower rail…

...and the upper side rail.

Before adding the bracing piece, hold the two sides together and adjust to match.

Add the bracing piece. Then double nail all the joints.

Take a moment to hold the sides up to check the match and envision the chair.

Though the ends of some rungs and rails will be accessible when the chair is finished, others will not. It is a good idea to clean up the ends of the rungs and rails with a rasp before they are installed.

Align the top rail with the outside of the upper side rail.

Progress.

Nail the seat rail in place, through the rail into the leg, bracing the chair with your leg and hand.

Add a third front rail under the side bracing piece.

Do the same thing on the lower front rail.

The chair should taper from about 20 inches in the front between the rails...

...to about 17″ in the back.

Add a back stretcher to hold the rear legs in place. It will overhang on each side.

With the bottom of the legs set also about 17″ apart at the inside of the lower side rail, nail the lower stretcher in place.

Turn the chair over and add a seat brace. It is attached to the undersides of the top side rails about 12″ behind the front legs.

Progress.

Add a second nail to the seat brace from the top for strength.

...and nail it in place.

Add a narrower 24" brace behind the front leg.

Progress.

The top rail is also about 1-1/4" in diameter and about 32" long. Center and situate the top rail...

Before adding the bending twigs, add some finishing touches are needed, like rasping the top of the front leg. It will soon be inaccessible.

Leaving about a finger's width protrusion, cut off the excess on the seat brace…

Rasp the ends of the rails.

…and the rail at the back of the seat.

Go back and double nail any joints that were missed before, like here at the lower back rail…

Do the same on the rail at the lower back.

…and here at the top. When you can get right angles they work together to give more strength to the joint.

The willow benders are about 3/4" in diameter. They should be worked "to get the spite out it." You push down and roll it as it bends. This compresses the fiber and causes it to get limber.

Insert the bender at the side in front of the back leg. It should go between the top rail and the brace and touch the floor.

Bend the stick so it touches the end of the back stretcher.

Brace the leg with your foot.

Curve it back in so it crosses the top rail about 5 inches outside the back leg. Nail it in place.

Use your body to bend the stick and nail to the back leg at about the level of the lower rail.

Start another bender from the other side, nailing into the bottom of the leg.

Bend it in the same way and nail it into the top rail.

Lay a second bender along side the first, nailing it into the side brace.

As you work your way up, nail the new bender into the one beside it.

Progress.

Repeat every 6" or so.

Nail into the top rail.

Continue nail the two benders together above the rail. The purpose is to help them form a flat surface.

In the same way add two more benders to each side for a total of four.

One side done. Move to the other side. It is good to alternate sides, and helps avoid excessive torque.

Continue nailing them together until about three feet above the top rail. As you move up, use longer nails so you can catch more of the benders.

Lay the chair on the ground to help keep the benders flat. Determine where you want the crossover. Three feet above the rail looks good.

Align the center.

Nail in place.

Nail at each intersection of benders.

Progress.

Trim the top.

The result.

The number of benders you use in the seat can vary, but it should always be an even number. An odd number would put one right in the middle which would bother your spine. Instead we'll work start with benders on either side of the center line and work our way out. Insert the bender through the back of the chair.

Holding the saw at an angle of the leg, cut off the lower ends of the benders.

Bend the stick by pushing it into place.

Align the first bender about 1" from the center line.

After the first bender is in, add a 3/4" piece on top of the top front rail and abutting the front legs.

Nail it to the brace under the seat....

Nail it in place.

...and again to the cross piece at the bottom of the chair back.

Working the other side of center add your second bender in the same way, and continue working your way out.

Bend them so the bottom of the seat is flat.

As you continue adding benders, keeping the spacing even.

When all the pieces are in place begin to work at the front of the seat to shape it. Pull the outside bender to the leg.

Mark where it needs to be cut to fit just behind the small piece added to the upper front rail.

Cut it on the mark.

Hold it in place and nail into the rail behind the front leg.

Spread the benders evenly...

Continue working your way across, cutting the benders to length...

and nail them in place.

So they fall in place just behind the front rail.

Move to the top rail. Add the bend you want to the outside bender and nail to the top rail.

Do the same to the outside bender on the other side. This sets your borders.

Trim the excess length of the benders, but don't go too short.

Now spread the remaining benders evenly at the top rail...

Bend the outside to a nice curve. Nail it in place, going into innermost back piece or the one next to it. Too close to the end will cause breakage later on.

...and nail in place.

Move to the other side and make a matching curve, then nail it in place.

Fan the five benders on one side out to visualize their placement.

Nail the benders, working on one while holding the next one in place. When all the benders are tacked in place, go back and add a second nail. This gives you an opportunity to add a little more movement to the fan.

With one side done, do the other to match.

Lop off the excess ends of the back benders.

Clean up the ends of the benders, rasping outward.

A wrap of bark is a nice finishing touch.

A Woven Willow Bark Lampshade

Jo Kilmer

Once while attending a Woodlanders Gathering, I heard a lot of people talking about how "trees talk to them" or "trees call to them." I believe the real art is being able to listen and hear what the trees have to say. There is definitely a deep connection with tree listeners and the trees and I feel blessed to have that connection.

I grew up in the small river town of Staatsburg, New York. Being the only girl with two brothers and a nickname like Jo, you can probably imagine I was a little tomboyish, spending lots of time climbing trees and building forts. Fortunately for me I have always had family and friends who have encouraged my talents. My dad told me once that "You can do anything you want to do, as long as you want it bad enough." That has always stuck with me.

I have been listening and working with trees full time for eleven years now. Along my journey in rustic furniture, I have found myself building everything from a miniature 4-inch chair to a pavilion made of locust and laurel. My newest endeavor is some very cool bark jewelry. Some of my work can be seen on Bim Willow's website www.rusticfurnituremakers.com and is also available at the Longbranch Gallery, Mineral Point Wisconsin and the Globe Gallery in Clayton Georgia. You can reach me at wovenbark@yahoo.com or by calling 828-837-4866.

Black willow is harvested when the sap is up in the tree, usually early summer. The leaves are out and the bark comes off easily. If you harvest is the winter the bark will not come off. The bark can be used green or dried then resoaked. If I know the project I am planning, I will cut it to particular length. Only use bark from the straight section of the tree. This bark has been dried so it needs to be resoaked. When you resoak, as opposed to using it green, much of the shrinkage has already occurred.

Soak the bark until it is pliable enough to use. It should bend without breaking. It usually takes about 24 hours. Warming the water to room temperature will help the process and it speeds up even more with hot water. Also, adding a little bit of mineral spirits to the warm water will help make the bark pliable.

While the bark is soaking I build the frame for the lampshade. For the ribs I will use 3/4" black willow twigs, cut to 18-1/2". This project requires two pieces for each side for a total of 8 ribs.

Sand the ends of all the twigs for a more finished look.

There are also three horizontal pieces for each side. The bottom piece is 18", the middle piece is 15-3/4", and the top piece is 2-1/4".

The result.

Cut the ends of the horizontal pieces at 30 degrees to fit in the pyramid shape of the panel.

Align the bottom cross piece about 1/2" from the bottom of the rib and drill a pilot hole.

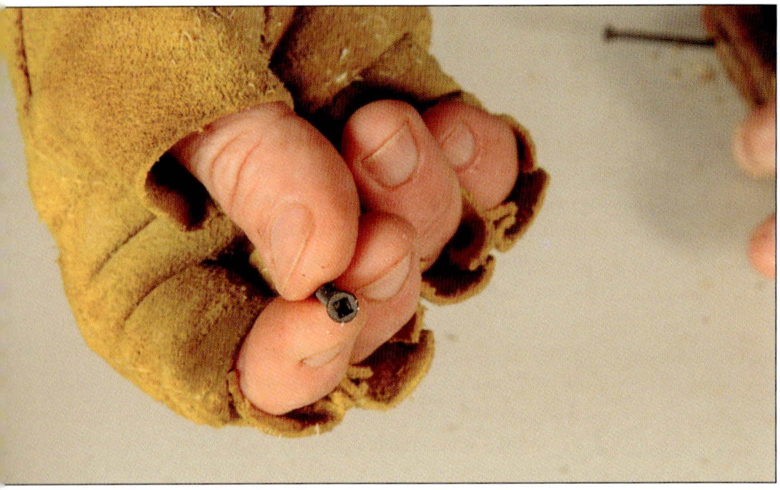

I use a trim head screw. This is 1-5/8″. The trim head countersinks itself and allows me to hide it.

Screw the lower cross piece in place.

Repeat on the other end of the cross piece—drill the pilot...

...and screw in place.

The bottom cross piece in place.

Align the top cross piece about 1/4″ from the top.

Drill the pilot.

Drive the screw...

...leaving some exposed. Going further would split the cross piece.

Before doing the other end, I need to flatten the area.

Attach the other side.

The frame is finished.

Align the middle cross piece.

Divide the lower cross piece in half ...

Drill a pilot and secure with a screw in the same way as before.

... and in half again, for four equal segments.

At each point, determine the size of the connector…

...and cut to length.

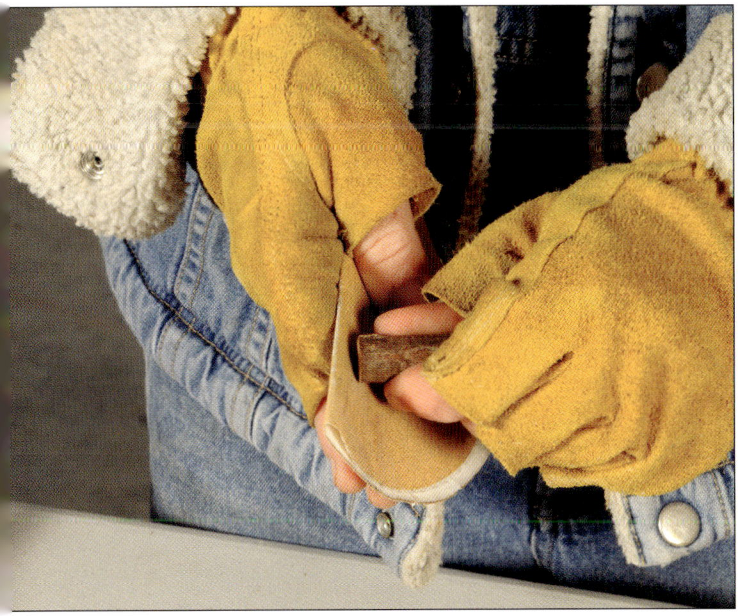

Sand the ends. I use 80 grit paper.

Position the piece and drill a pilot hole.

Secure with a finishing nail. I move the piece to a corner of the table for support.

Do the same for all the vertical trim pieces.

Do the same from the top. Drill a pilot...

The vertical trim pieces in place.

...and secure with a nail.

Another trim piece goes from corner to corner in the segments of the lower area. Hold the diagonal trim piece in place and mark one end. You want the point to go into the corner and the angle to be against the cross piece.

Cut.

Secure with one inch brads. I drill the pilot down through the diagonal into the cross piece at an angle.

Hold the cut end place and mark the other end.

Nail in place.

Cut and check the fit.

Trim off the nail head.

Progress.

and second along the cross piece.

Continue with the other panels in the same way.

Cut the rib angle first…

In the end segments, the corner diagonal is cut in two directions. First along the rib..

...then the horizontal angle.

On this piece I secure from outside of the rib, drilling a pilot first...

Ready to weave. Prepare all four panels like this.

...and nailing. Like before, nail the other end down into the lower cross piece. Repeat at the other end.

The soaked bark can now be prepared for weaving. I begin by sanding the surface with an orbital sander, using 80 grit paper.

Cut off the nails at the top piece.

The result. I am not trying to get a perfectly smooth surface, but one that is uniform and pleasing to the eye and touch.

Brush away the debris.

Wipe down the back with mineral spirits. This takes off dust and funguses that may have collected.

When it is all cleaned, cut the bark into 1-1/4" strips. Exact sizes are not important, and in fact may detract from the rustic look.

A stockpile is ready for work.

Working from the back of the panel frame, align the middle piece of bark, rough side down, and staple in place at the top.

Working out, lay the next piece in place and trim to fit the corner. Staple one piece on each side of the center.

Lay out the remaining pieces on one side...

...and the other.

Tack in place at the top. I staple across the grain so it doesn't pull out.

Ready to weave.

Still working from the back, the first piece goes under the center and over the two side pieces.

From there the pattern goes two over, two under, working down the panel. Always count your weave from the same edge.

When all are in place, go back and tighten up the weave. This will probably involve removing the tacking staple, but the weave should now be sturdy enough to hold its shape.

Tighten the weave.

Check the lines from the front.

Staple the bark to the middle cross piece. The staple overlaps the joints to help keep the bark ends from curling while drying.

Tap the staples in with a hammer on the cross piece and at the top. These will be covered.

On the spines I tack the bark to the wood, using No. 8 tacks because they are not too big. Remove the staples.

Drive the tacks so they are toward the center of the panel. This leaves room to trim the excess bark.

I usually use two tacks in each piece of bark.

Ready for trimming.

You can trim the edge off with a knife…

Cut a strip from a piece of scrap to cover the stapled ends at the top and bottom.

…or a cutting disc.

Trim to fit…

This produces a nice, finished edge.

…and tack in place. Repeat on the bottom.

The back side is finished.

Cut it out.

On the front side there is a decorative medallion pattern at the top. I lay a piece of paper on the panel to make the design.

Glue the medallion in place using wood glue.

Cut out the pattern and transfer it to a piece of bark.

Using a piece of 1x cut to shape to even the pressure, clamp the bark in place until the glue dries.

Mark and cut a trim piece for the bottom edge of the medallion.

Where the two trim pieces meet, they are toe-nailed together, by drilling a pilot...

Drill a pilot from outside the rib...

...and driving a nail.

...and nail in place. Do the same from the other side.

The result. Repeat on all four panels of the lampshade.

When the four panels are done, we are ready for assembly. Align two sides at right angles. Drill a pilot hole...

...and screw them together. I use a screw with a head, which helps pull the ribs together.

Look for places where the wood touches and put screws there. I end up with about three screws on a side.

Trim off a high point if it gets too much in the way.

Add another side.

An 1-1/2″ piece, sliced in half, is used as the top bracket.

Measure across the top of the lampshade and mark.

Cut one end at 45 degrees.

Cut the other end to fit.

Holding the bracket in place, drill a pilot through the top cross piece...

...and screw it in place with a headless trim screw. For strength, use two on each end of the bracket.

Drill a hole in the center for the wire nipple.

Add the hardware and it is ready to hang.

As a finishing touch, I use brown wood putty to fill the holes.

With some coloration of the medallion and the addition of some feather embellishments, the lampshade is complete.

A Ladderback Chair

Veronica Chenier

I always loved the smell of wood; new wood, old wood, sawdust. The feel of wood, its voice, even the slivers. It's the slivers that teach you respect. It wasn't until a four day workshop in November, 1984, that I truly began my rustic journey towards today.

My style grains towards a more refined rustic and some gentle hints of free-form branch work. With my background in drawing, design, and sign printing, I often like to incorporate my wood carvings, burnings, or artwork into a piece. Found objects, iron miscellany, or nature's droppings are added when the wood invites it.

Home is the Ottawa Valley, Ontario, Canada. This is a low lying area conducive to the growth of most of my basic wood supplies. When I'm finished my part time day job as a baker, I take my tools, rubber boots and head out to the woods and pastures and heaven.

The freeform ladderback chair I am making will use fresh cut, white birch for all parts except the seat and some of the decorative back pieces. These will be willow. I use spiral finishing nails or paneling nails. The legs are about 1-1/2" in diameter. After determining where the bottom of the back leg should be, cut the bottom end flat to floor. I like to use fairly straight back legs because it simplifies the mortise and tenon application for the four horizontal rungs.

Measure up 55" from the bottom.

I use green chalk to mark on birch.

Go about 6″ inches above the mark for the cut.
This extra Is needed for the angle cut.

Cut.

On the other back leg repeat the same basic steps.
Cut the bottom.

For this leg, measure up 45" and mark.

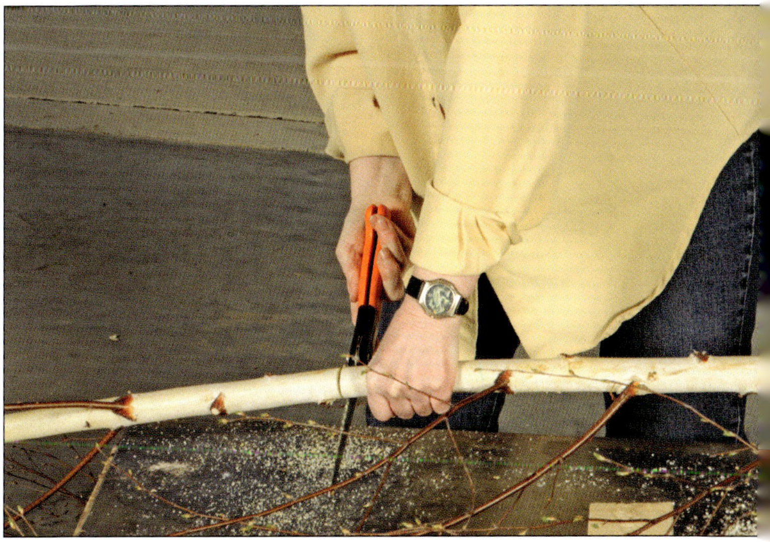

Go 6″ higher and cut.

Place the legs side by side to visualize. The smaller, middle branches can stay and might be incorporated into the design. In this position some will jut into the sitter's back so I'll turn the legs over.

Now I can see which branches to trim and which to keep.

Begin by removing most of the outside branches. I'll trim some of the inside branches after I've gotten a little further along and can be sure which I want to keep.

Progress. I've left a couple of "maybe" branches on the outside in case I want to wrap them around and work them into the design.

Mark the bottom ends of the legs with a vertical line to preserve their position. If they roll you will be able to re-align them to the desired position.

At the top of the leg, cut a 45 degree angle from the back, toward the measure line on the front.

You can now remove inside branches that you know you're not going to use.

Rasp around the angled cut to clean it up.

Do the same on the other leg. You can use a lopper instead of a saw especially if the wood is green. Rasp ends as you complete them.

Measure up 18" from the bottom of both legs and mark. This will be the top of the seat, which is started later on.

Starting above the 18" seat line, lay out your pattern for the ladder rungs. I work on one end of each rung first, leaving lots of length for unexpected problems.

As you consider the pattern, remember that you will be mortising the rungs into the legs. Situate them so that branches or knots will not interfere with this. I like this 2+2 pattern. Important: keep both legs flush to the edge of your worktable as if they're sitting on the floor.

At this point, too, you decide how far apart the back legs will be. I want them 8-1/2" apart, and parallel from bottom to top.

The overall length of the rung will be 9" to 9-1/2". Each tenon end will be 1/2" to 3/4" long. Measure...

...and cut.

This half-inch tenon cutter fits into a power drill.

The rungs sometimes don't fit into the mouth of the cutter, so they need to be carved down a bit.

Align the rung straight with the cutter and cut it. I do only one end first, the thickest, so I have excess if I run into a splitting or knot problem.

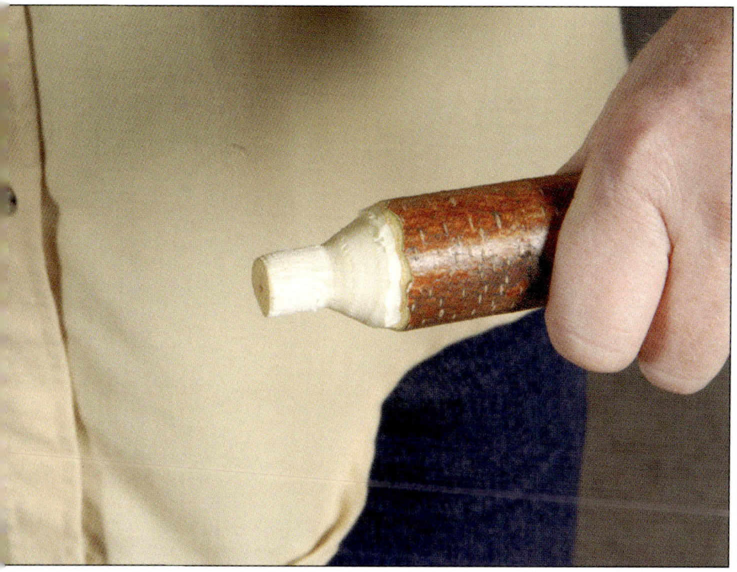

I want about an 3/4" tenon.

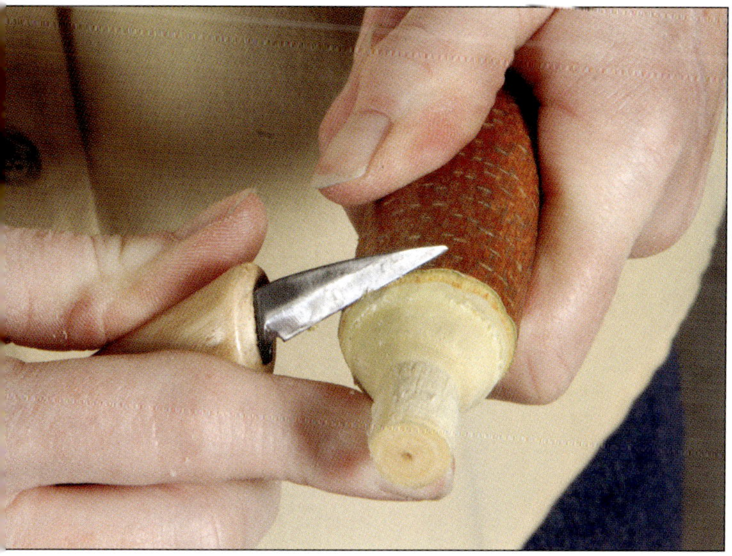

Clean up the edge around the bark.

Trim one end of each rung.

From the butt of the tenon, measure 9" and mark. This will be the butt of the other tenon.

Go 3/4" or so beyond that mark and cut the rung.

Make the tenon.

The rungs are ready.

From tenon butt to tenon butt it is 8-1/2".

Align the feet with a straight edge, like this tabletop. Check that your marks on the feet bottom are still vertical to the table.

Use the first rung as a template to cut the others.

Place the rungs at the spots decided upon earlier. In this case (2+2) the lower rungs are centered on 25" & 29" from the floor.

The next rung is centered on 39″.

The top rung is at 43″.

Mark the locations with chalk on the inside of one leg.

Check that all the points are in a straight line.

Drill the mortises about 3/4″ deep.

Insert the rungs in one side.

Sometimes a block under the pressure point really helps the hammering.

Make the mortises.

Mark the other leg using the same measurements. Check that these points are also in a straight line.

Dry fit the two sides. The rungs may need to be turned so they won't press into the sitter's back.

Before drilling the second side, double check by aligning the rungs with the dots.

Because of the slight curve of one leg, the middle two rungs are a bit long.

The easiest adjustment for this is to deepen the mortises for those tenons.

Continue with the dry fitting. Alternate thick and thin ends, left, right for visual balance.

With the back legs dry fit, check for straightness.

Disassemble the ladder back and apply glue to the mortises and tenons.

With one side glued, do the other. Try to get the decorative branches in their final position.

On the outside of the leg, opposite the top rung, cut a small flap in the bark for a screw.

Screw through the leg into the tenon end of the rung. Do this on the other leg too.

Add a dab of glue…

…and replace the flap. Do the same at each end of the bottom rung.

The ladder complete.

On the back of the ladder measure up 18″ from the floor. A 15″ seat rail will be placed here, its top edge no higher than the 18″ mark.

The lower rail on the back is set so its top edge is 6″ above the floor. These pieces are never perfectly straight, so I make it a practice to alternate thick and thin ends. The lower rail has the thick end on the right; the upper has it on the left.

Nail the rails in place. Use that block of wood under the impact point. Your hands will thank you.

Check for straightness and balance.

Trim the wood for the front legs...

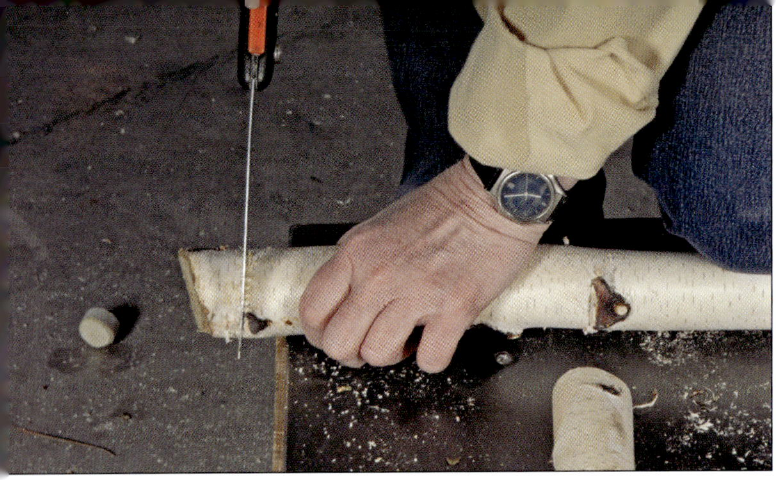

...and square the foot. Cut the length of the front legs to 20″.

As always clean up the ends with a rasp.

The front legs will be wider apart than the back...between 18″ and 22″, though they can be any width you like. In this case I will be making them 18″ apart.

At the front there are three rails, about 24″ long, 2 at the top, 1 at the bottom. Cut to length, lay in place to visualize.

The top edge of the lower rail is 6″ above the foot, as was done on the back legs.

The top edge of the uppermost rail is 18″ above the foot.

Do the same on the top rail. The other front rail will be done later.

Sometimes there is a knot or branch stub that needs to be leveled for a good fit.

Eyeball it for levelness and squareness before hammering the nails all the way in.

Realign, measure, and nail the bottom rail in place.

Add a second nail, slightly offset from the first. Putting in two nails, close together along the same grain line invites splitting so move it slightly away and up or down from first.

The side rails are 22″ long. Situate the side rail outside of the legs and under the upper rail in the front and its coordinating rail in the back. Tie it in place for now.

As steady as possible, hold the front leg section near its final position relative to the back. A second set of hands is helpful. Nail the upper side rail in place…into the front leg…

…and the back leg.

Repeat on the other side.

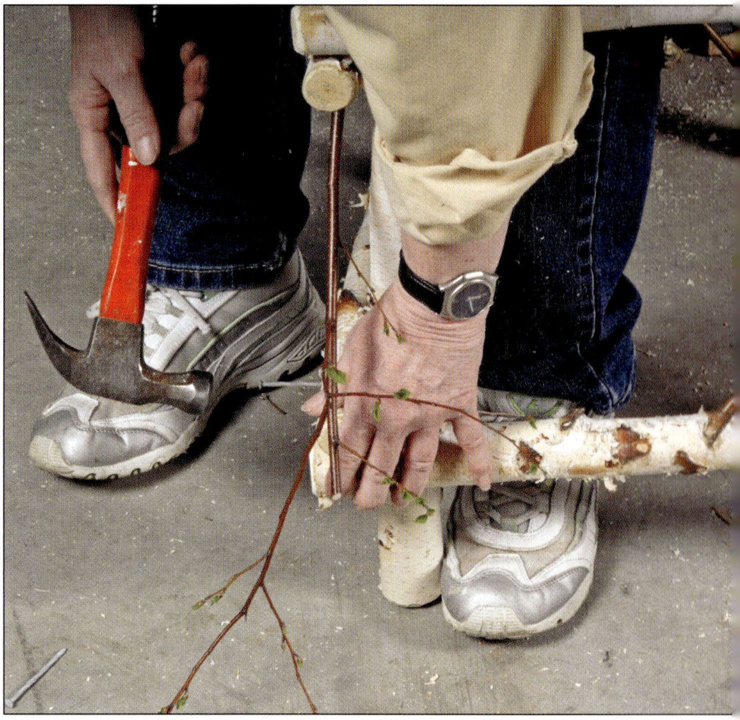

Carefully check the alignment and adjust before nailing the lower rails in place.

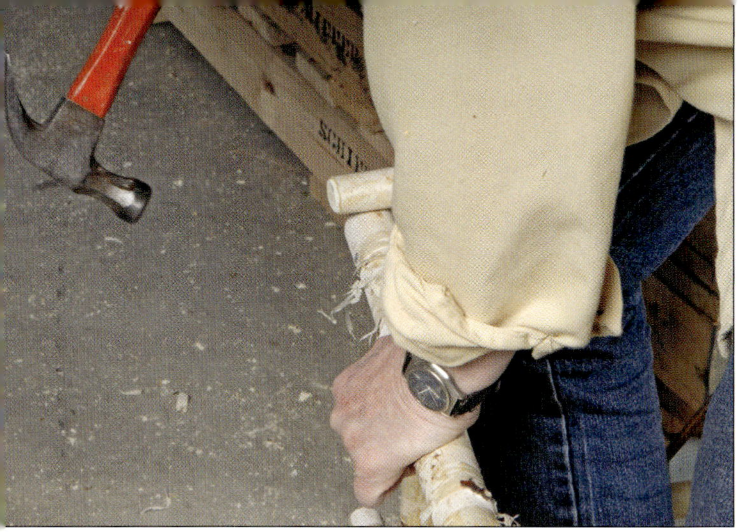

When all is good, go back and add a second nail to the side rail joints.

The frame complete.

Align the middle front rail so it comes under the upper side rail. Turn it until you get a pleasing effect…

…then nail in place.

Nail any small branches you've left on, where they cross the main members of the frame. I use small, ribbed 1" paneling nails for this minute work. Surprisingly, these decorative branches do add to the chair's stability.

On each side, a brace runs diagonally from outside the front leg, just under the side rail...

...to inside the back leg above the lower rail.

Add two braces across the seat. One at the front...

...and one near the back. I like a little bow in this one to provide a better fit for the human form.

Nail the braces in place. I used 1-5/8" spiral paneling nails.

The seat is formed with willow benders. They should be cut to fit from the back rail to the front rail. I use the thicker segments on the outside, because they don't bend.

Fan the twigs out to form the seat.

Nail the outer most one or two on each side then nail the middle bender.

Fill in the area between, keeping the spaces even.

The benders in place.

Cut a top piece to fit the front of the seat, above the top rail.

This goes under the knees so needs to be quite smooth for comfort's sake.

Nail it in place into the front legs. To leave some elasticity, I don't nail in the middle.

Cut a thinner piece to go between the front legs and cover the ends of the benders.

Nail it in place.

Also add a piece to cover the bender ends at the back of the seat.

Trim off the smaller branches now as they would break off anyway. They are too small to keep.

Use double pronged tacks to hold some of the more slender branches in place.

Adding birch and/or willow branches to the back of the chair in this fashion creates a free form movement. Fasten with tacks or nails as required.

Tack the trimmed branches in place with a fine, small nail.

Wind some of the flexible small branches around the lower supports. These are held in place with double-pronged tacks. Now sit down, lean back and rest in your chair. You deserve it.

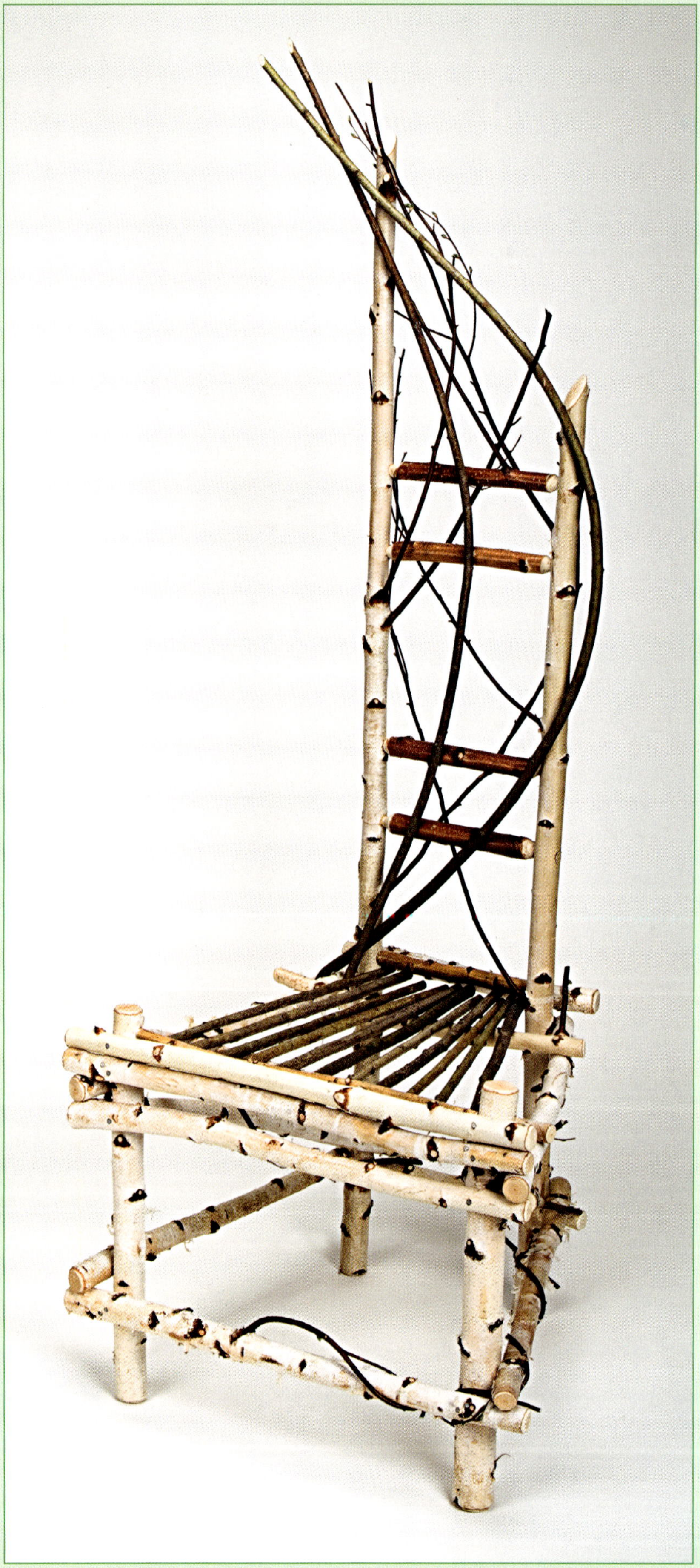

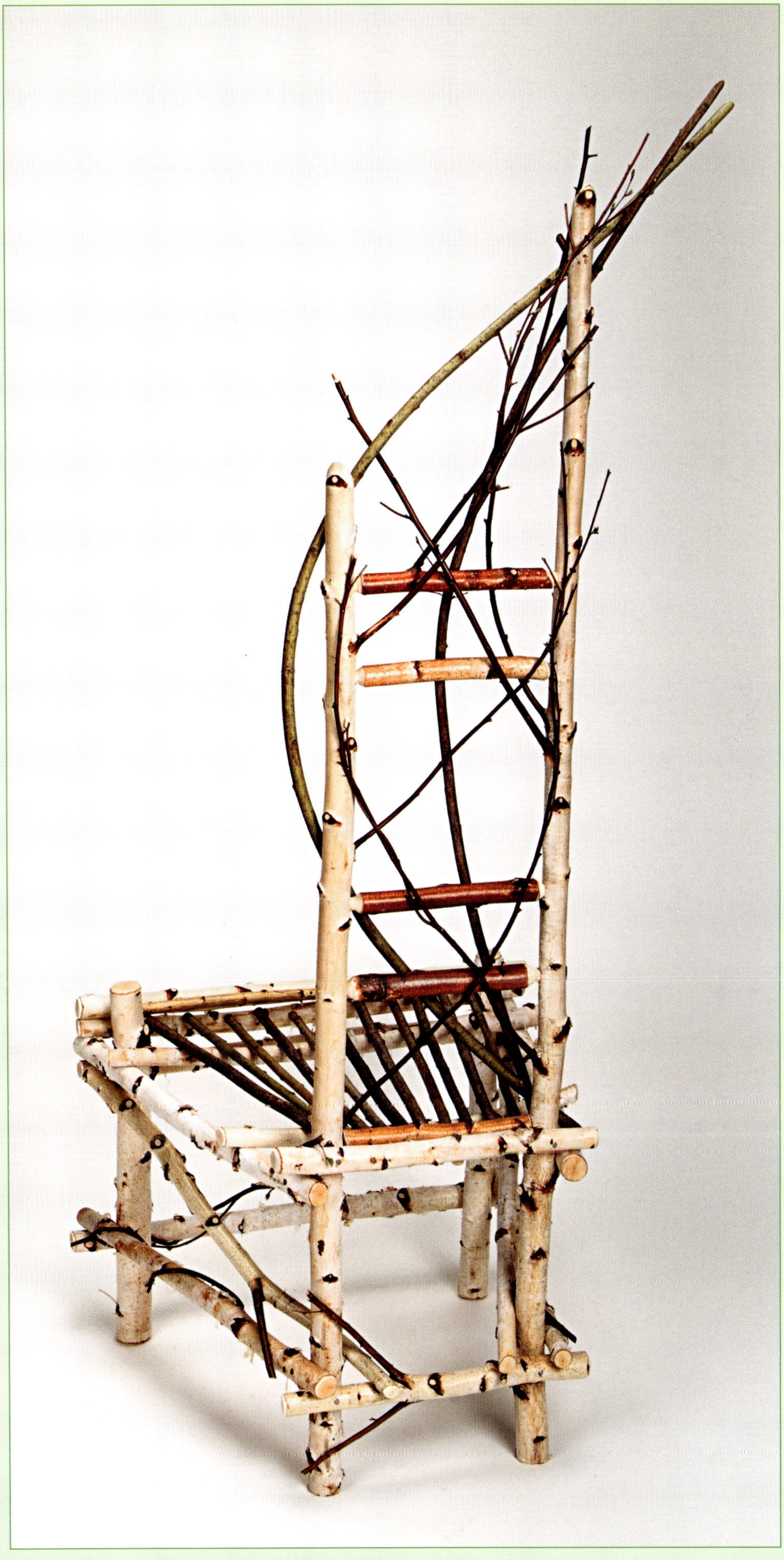

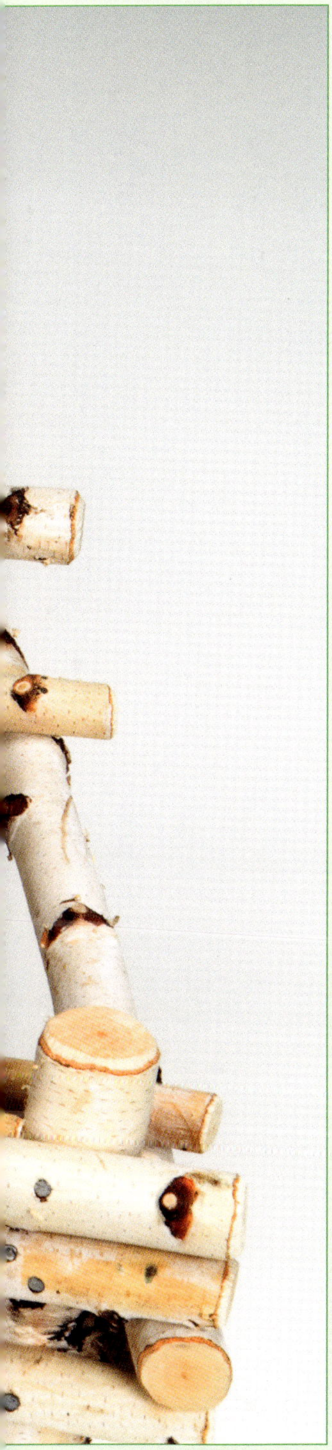